2015

HEALTH INSURANCE FRAUDS

AN OVERVIEW

Adnan Mastan

BUMS, MD (Medicine),

FIII, DHI, DHM, DLU

HEALTH INSURANCE FRAUDS

Name of the Book: Health Insurance Frauds

Name of the Author: Dr.Adnan Mastan

Published: August 2015

Edition: First

Note: As new information becomes available, changes become necessary. The editors/author/contributors have, as far as it is possible, taken care to ensure that the information given in this book is accurate and up-to-date. In view of the possibility of human error or advances in medical science neither the author nor the publisher nor any other party who has been involved in the preparation or publication of this work warrants that the information contained herein is in every respect accurate or complete. Readers are strongly advised to confirm.

Printed in USA

Dedicated to

My Mother

for his constant encouragement and support

"Victory lies in every step, not at the end of the race alone"

Preface

Health insurance industry is growing and being chanted about like the new mantra, but, still India is facing a huge loss in this sector because of the everyday increasing fraud claims. This book is aimed to provide concise introduction of the health insurance frauds along with specific mention to basic approaches to combat health insurance frauds. It is hoped that this book shall provide evidence based guidelines about health insurance frauds to all readers.

I am highly indebted to my friends and colleagues for providing the necessary stimulus for writing this book. I am grateful to all those persons whose writings and works have helped me in the preparation of this book. I am equally grateful to the reviewer of the manuscript of this book who made extremely valuable suggestions and has thus contributed in enhancing the standard of the book. I shall feel amply rewarded if the book proves helpful to the readers. I look forward to suggestions from all readers for further improving the subject content as well as the presentation of this book.

Adnan Mastan

Contents

Introduction ……………..…………………………….……..……… 1

Health Insurance …………………………………..……..……... 6

Health Insurance Scenario In Other Countries …………..……....…... 9

Review of Literature …………………………………..…….. 16

Cashless Hospitalization Facility…………………………..…….. 23

Stake Holders in Health Insurance …….…..….……....…….….. 28

Health Insurance Frauds ………..…………………...…………... 32

Types of Health Insurance Frauds ……………..…………....…….. 34

Triggers of Health Insurance Frauds ……………………………. 38

Managing Frauds ………………...…………………..…….…... 42

IPC & Indian Contract Act ……………………..…………....……... 51

Protocols For Level Of Misconduct/Fraud ………………..…...…... 58

Conclusion ……………………………………………………... 64

Attributes Of An Investigator ……………………..…..…………… 66

Annexure…………………………………..……………….…... 67

INTRODUCTION

The term health insurance is generally used to describe a form of insurance that pays for medical expenses. It is sometimes used more broadly to include insurance covering disability or long-term nursing or custodial care needs. It may be provided through a government-sponsored social insurance program, or from private insurance companies. It may be purchased on a group basis (e.g., by a firm to cover its employees) or purchased by individual consumers. In each case, the covered groups or individuals pay premiums or taxes to help protect themselves from high or unexpected healthcare expenses. Similar benefits paying for medical expenses may also be provided through social welfare programs funded by the government. Health insurance works by estimating the overall risk of healthcare expenses and developing a routine finance structure (such as a monthly premium or annual tax) that will ensure that money is available to pay for the healthcare benefits specified in the insurance agreement. The benefit is administered by a central organization, most often either a government agency or a private or not-for-profit entity operating a health plan.

Health Insurance in India: Current Scenario

The health care system in India is characterized by multiple systems of Medicine, mixed ownership patterns and different kinds of delivery structures. Public sector ownership is divided between central and state governments, Municipal and *Panchayat* local governments. Public health facilities include Teaching hospitals, secondary level hospitals, first-level referral hospitals (CHCs or rural hospitals), dispensaries; primary health centres (PHCs), sub-centres, and health posts. Also included are public facilities for selected occupational Groups like organized work force (ESI), defence, government employees (CGHS), railways, post and telegraph and mines among others. The private sector (for profit and not for profit) is the dominant sector with 50 per cent of people seeking indoor care and around 60 to 70 per cent of those seeking ambulatory care (or outpatient care) from private health facilities. While India has made significant gains in terms of health indicators- demographic, infrastructural and epidemiological.

This is coupled with spiraling health costs, high financial burden on the poor and erosion in their incomes. Around 24% of all people hospitalized in India in a single year fall below the poverty line due to hospitalization *(World Bank, 2002)*. An analysis of financing of hospitalization shows that large proportion of people; especially those in the bottom for income quintiles borrow money or sell assets to pay for hospitalization *(World Bank, 2002)* This situation exists in a scenario where health care is financed through general tax revenue, community financing, out of pocket payment and social and private health insurance schemes. India spends about 4.9% of GDP on *(Regional Overview in South-East Asia)* health *(WHR, 2002)*. The per capita total expenditure on health in India is US$ 23, of which the per capita Government expenditure on health is US$ 4.Hence, it is seen that the total health expenditure is around 5% of GDP, with breakdown of public expenditure (0.9%); private expenditure (4.0%). The private expenditure can be further classified as out-of-pocket (OOP) expenditure (3.6%) and employees/community financing (0.4%). It is thus evident that public health investment has been comparatively low. In fact as a percentage of GDP it has declined from 1.3% in 1990 to 0.9% as at present. Furthermore, the central budgetary allocation for health (as a percentage of the total Central budget) has been stagnant at 1.3% while in the states it has declined from 7.0% to 5.5%.

Table 1. Socioeconomic indicators

Land area	2% of world area
Burden of disease (%)	21% of global disease burden
Population	16% of world population
Urban : Rural	28:72
Literacy rate (%)	65.38
Sanitation (%)	Rural – 9.0; Urban – 49.3
Safe drinking water supply (%)	Rural – 98; Urban – 90.2
Poverty (%)	Below poverty line – 26
	Rural – 27.09; Urban – 23.62
Poverty line (Rs.)	Rural – 327.56; Urban – 454.11

Table 2. Achievements: 1951-2000

Demographic changes	1951	1981	2000
Life expectancy	36.7	54	64.6 (RGI)
Crude birth rate	40.8	33.9 (SRS)	26.1 (99 SRS)
Crude death rate	25	12.5 (SRS)	8.7 (99 SRS)
Infant mortality rate	146	110	70 (99 SRS)

Epidemiology	1951	1981	2000
Malaria (cases in million)	75	2.7	2.2
Leprosy cases per 10,000 Population	38.1	57.3	3.74
Small pox (no of cases)	>44,887	Eradicated	Eradicated
Guinea worm (no. of cases)	>39,792	Eradicated	Eradicated
Polio		29709	265

Infrastructure	1951	1981	2000
SC/PHC/CHC	725	57,363	1,63,181(99-RHS)
Dispensaries & hospitals(all)	9209	23,555	43,322 (95–96-CBHI)
Beds (Pvt & Public)	117,198	569,495	8,70,161 (95-96-CBHI)
Doctors (Allopathy)	61,800	2,68,700	5,03,900 (98-99-MCI)
Nursing personnel	18,054	1,43,887	7,37,000 (99-INC)

In light of the fiscal crisis facing the government at both central and state levels, in the form of shrinking public health budgets, escalating health care costs coupled with demand for health-care services, and lack of easy access of people from the low-income group to quality health care, health insurance is emerging as an alternative mechanism for financing of health care.

HEALTH INSURANCE

Health insurance in a narrow sense would be 'an individual or group purchasing health care coverage in advance by paying a fee called *premium*.' In its broader sense, it would be any arrangement that helps to defer, delay, reduce or altogether avoid payment for health care incurred by individuals and households. The health insurance market in India is very limited covering about 10% of the total population. The existing schemes can be categorized as:

1. Voluntary health insurance schemes or private-for-profit schemes;

2. Employer-based schemes;

3. Insurance offered by NGOs / community based health insurance, and

4. Mandatory health insurance schemes or government run schemes (namely ESIS, CGHS).

Need for Health Insurance

Health care costs are rising rapidly. Today, the best health care involves high cost technologies that latest advancements in medical field facilitate. Added to this is the expertise of professionals, and utilities. A citizen has to pay huge fees to avail such health care. Low and middle-income people who are not prepared to pay for their emergency health care expenses, during an unforeseen accident or major illness, find health insurance a viable alternative.

Health insurance helps in ensuring that no one is deprived of the minimum health care. Its primary aim is to protect a patient and his family from financial disaster and simplifying the mode of payments. For example, instead of making separate payments, say for the doctors, surgeon, pathologist, nurse etc., the insured will pay premium to the insurer who in turn will take care of all these expenses. It also helps in eliminating sickness as a cause of poverty and helps reduce anxieties of different nature – economic, medical and moral. Health insurance companies thus provide financial assistance to the insured in case of disability or loss of health, so that he/she can take curative measures and also maintain their dependents during the period of sickness/disability with the benefits the insurer provides.

Health insurance is classified into three categories:

1. Medical Expense Insurance: The expenses of the insured, such as hospital, physician and other health care expenses are covered by this arrangement.

2. Disability Income Insurance: Disability income policies replace lost income when the insured is disabled as a result of sickness or injury. Payment is made because physical or mental incapacity prevents the insured from working.

3. Long-term Care Insurance: Long-term insurance policies promise to pay expenses if the incapacity prohibits the insured's activities of daily life.

Voluntary health insurance schemes or private-for-profit schemes

In private insurance, buyers are willing to pay premium to an insurance company that pools people with similar risks and insures them for health expenses. The key distinction is that the premiums are set at a level, which provides a profit to third party and provider institutions. Premiums are based on an assessment of the risk status of the consumer (or of the group of employees) and the level of benefits provided, rather than as a proportion of the consumer's income.

In the public sector, the General Insurance Corporation (GIC) and its four subsidiary companies (National Insurance Corporation, New India Assurance Company, Oriental Insurance Company and United Insurance Company) and the Life Insurance Corporation (LIC) of India provide voluntary insurance schemes.

Of the various schemes offered, Mediclaim is the main product of the GIC. The Medical Insurance Scheme or Med claim was introduced in November 1986 and it covers individuals and groups with persons aged 5 – 80 yrs. Children (3 months – 5 yrs) are covered with their parents. This scheme provides for reimbursement of medical expenses (now offers cashless scheme) by an individual towards hospitalization and domiciliary hospitalization as per the sum insured. There are exclusions and pre-existing disease clauses. Premiums are calculated based on age and the sum insured, which in turn varies from Rs 15 000 to Rs 5 00 000. In 1995/96 about half a million Mediclaim policies were issued with about 1.8 million beneficiaries (Krause Patrick 2000). The coverage for the year 2000-01 was around 7.2 million.

The year 1999 marked the beginning of a new era for health insurance in the Indian context. With the passing of the Insurance Regulatory Development Authority Bill (IRDA) the insurance sector was opened to private and foreign participation, thereby paving the way for the entry of private health insurance companies. The Bill also facilitated the establishment of an authority to protect the interests of the insurance holders by regulating, promoting and ensuring orderly growth of the insurance industry. The bill allows foreign promoters to hold paid up capital of up to 26 percent in an Indian company and requires them to have a capital of Rs 100 crore along with a business plan to begin its operations. Currently, a few companies such as Bajaj Alliance, ICICI, Royal Sundaram, and Cholamandalam among others are offering health insurance schemes. Karnataka 7 000 Health Insurance

HEALTH INSURANCE SCENARIO IN OTHER COUNTRIES

Health insurance in Australia

The public health system is called Medicare. It ensures free universal access to hospital treatment and subsidized out-of-hospital medical treatment. It is funded by a 1.5% tax levy.

The private health system is funded by a number of private health insurance organizations. The largest of these is Medibank Private, which is government-owned, but operates as a government business enterprise under the same regulatory regime as all other registered private health funds. The Coalition Howard government had announced that Medibank would be privatized if it won the 2007 election, however they were defeated by the Australian Labor Party under Kevin Rudd which had already pledged that it would remain in government ownership.

Some private health insurers are 'for profit' enterprises, and some are non-profit organizations such as HCF Health Insurance. Some have membership restricted to particular groups, but the majority has open membership.

Most aspects of private health insurance in Australia are regulated by the *Private Health Insurance Act 2007*.

The private health system in Australia operates on a "community rating" basis, whereby premiums do not vary solely because of a person's previous medical history, current state of health or (generally speaking) their age (but see Lifetime Health Cover below). Balancing this are waiting periods, in particular for pre-existing conditions (usually referred to within the industry as PEA, which stands for "pre-existing ailment"). Funds are entitled to impose a waiting period of up to 12 months on benefits for any medical condition the signs and symptoms of which existed during the six months ending on the day the person first took out insurance. They are also entitled to impose a 12-month waiting period for benefits for treatment relating to an obstetric condition, and a 2-month waiting period for all other benefits when a person first takes out private insurance. Funds have the discretion to reduce or remove such waiting periods in individual cases. They are also free not to impose them to begin with, but this would place such a fund at risk of "adverse selection", attracting a disproportionate number of members from other funds, or from the pool of intending members who might otherwise have joined other funds. It would also attract people with existing medical conditions, who might not otherwise have taken out insurance at all because of the denial of benefits for 12 months due to the PEA Rule. The benefits paid out for these conditions would create pressure on premiums for all the fund's members, causing some to drop their membership, which would lead to further rises, and a vicious cycle would ensue.

There are a number of other matters about which funds are not permitted to discriminate between members in terms of premiums, benefits or membership - these include racial origin, religion, sex, sexual orientation, nature of employment, and leisure activities. Premiums for a fund's product that is sold in more than one state can vary from state to state, but not within the same state.

The Australian government has introduced a number of incentives to encourage adults to take out private hospital insurance. These include:

- **Lifetime Health Cover**: If a person has not taken out private hospital cover by the 1st July after their 30th birthday, then when (and if) they do so after this time, their premiums must include a loading of 2% per annum. Thus, a person taking out private cover for the first time at age 40 will pay a 20 per cent loading. The loading continues for 10 years. The loading applies only to premiums for hospital cover, not to ancillary (extras) cover.

- **Medicare Levy Surcharge**: People whose taxable income is greater than a specified amount (currently $50,000 for singles and $100,000 for families) and who do not have an adequate level of private hospital cover must pay a 1% surcharge on top of the standard 1.5% Medicare Levy. The rationale is that if the people in this income group are forced to pay more money one way or another, most would choose to purchase hospital insurance with it, with the possibility of a benefit in the event that they need private hospital treatment - rather than pay it in the form of extra tax as well as having to meet their own private hospital costs.

- **Private Health Insurance Rebate**: The government subsidizes the premiums for all private health insurance cover, including hospital and ancillary (extras), by 30%, 35% or 40%.

Health insurance in Canada

Most health insurance in Canada is administered by each province, under the Canada Health Act, which requires all people to have free access to basic health services. Collectively, the public provincial health insurance systems in Canada are frequently referred to as Medicare. Private health insurance is allowed, but the provincial governments allow it only for services that the public health plans do not cover; for example, semi-private or private rooms in hospitals and prescription drug plans. Canadians are free to use private insurance for elective medical services such as laser vision correction surgery, cosmetic surgery, and other non-basic medical procedures. Some 65% of Canadians have some form of supplementary private health insurance; many of them receive it through their employers. Private-sector services not paid for by the government account for nearly 30 percent of total health care spending. In 2005, the Supreme Court of Quebec ruled, in Chaoulli v. Quebec, that the province's prohibition on private insurance for health care already insured by the provincial plan could constitute an infringement of the right to life and security if there were long wait times for treatment as happened in this case. Certain other provinces have legislation which financially discourages but does not forbid private health insurance in areas covered by the public plans. The ruling has not changed the overall pattern of health insurance across Canada but has spurred on attempts to tackle the core issues of supply and demand and the impact of wait times.

Health insurance in the Netherlands

In the Netherlands in 2006, a new system of health insurance came into force. All insurance companies have to provide at least one policy which meets a government set minimum standard level of cover and all adult residents are obliged by law to purchase this cover from an insurance company of their choice.

The new system avoids the two pitfalls of adverse selection and moral hazard associated with traditional forms of health insurance.

In the Dutch system, insurance companies are compensated for taking on high risk individuals because they receive extra funding for them. This funding comes from an insurance equalization pool run by a regulator which collects salary based contributions from employers (about 45% of all health care funding) and funding from the government for people whose means are such that they cannot afford health care (about 5% of all funding). Thus insurance companies find that insuring high risk individuals becomes an attractive proposition. All insurance companies receive from the pool, but those with more high risk individuals will receive more from the fund. The remaining 45% of health care funding comes from insurance premiums paid by the public. Insurance companies compete for this money on price alone. The insurance companies are not allowed to set down any co-payments or caps or deductibles. Neither are they allowed to deny coverage to any person applying for a policy nor charge anything other than their nationally set and internet published standard policy premiums. Every person buying insurance from that company will pay the same price as everyone else buying that policy. And every person will get the minimum level of coverage. Children under 18 are insured for free (the funding coming from the equalization pool).

In addition to this minimum level, companies are free to sell extra insurance for additional coverage over the national minimum, but extra risks for this are not covered from the insurance pool and must therefore be priced accordingly.

Health insurance in the United Kingdom

Great Britain's National Health Service (NHS) is a publicly funded healthcare system that provides coverage to everyone normally resident in the UK. The NHS provides the majority of health care in England, including primary care, in-patient care, long-term health care, ophthalmology and dentistry. Private health care has continued parallel to the NHS, paid for largely by private insurance, but it is used by less than 8% of the population, and generally as a top-up to NHS services. Recently the private sector has been increasingly used to increase NHS capacity despite a large proportion of the British public opposing such involvement. According to the World Health Organization, government funding covered 86% of overall health care expenditures in the UK as of 2004, with private expenditures covering the remaining 14%. The costs of running the NHS (est. £104 billion in 2007-8) are met directly from general taxation. The National Health Service Act 1946 came into effect on 5 July 1948. The UK government department responsible for the NHS is the Department of Health, headed by a Secretary of State for Health (Health Secretary), who sits in the British Cabinet. The NHS is the world's largest health service and the world's third largest employer after the Chinese army and the Indian railways.

Health insurance in the United States

The US market-based health care system relies heavily on private and not-for-profit health insurance, which is the primary source of coverage for most Americans. According to the United States Census Bureau, approximately 84% of Americans have health insurance; some 60% obtain it through an employer, while about 9% purchase it directly. Various government agencies provide coverage to about 27% of Americans (there is some overlap in these figures).

Public programs provide the primary source of coverage for most seniors and for low-income children and families who meet certain eligibility requirements. The primary public programs are Medicare, a federal social insurance program for seniors and certain disabled individuals, Medicaid, funded jointly by the federal government and states but administered at the state level, which covers certain very low income children and their families, and SCHIP, also a federal-state partnership that serves certain children and families who do not qualify for Medicaid but who cannot afford private coverage. Other public programs include military health benefits provided through TRICARE and the Veterans Health Administration and benefits provided through the Indian Health Service. Some states have additional programs for low-income individuals.

In 2006, there were 47 million people in the United States (16% of the population) who were without health insurance for at least part of that year. About 37% of the uninsured live in households with an income over $50,000.

In 2004, US health insurers directly employed almost 470,000 people at an average salary of $61,409. (As of the fourth quarter of 2007, the total US labor force stood at 153.6 million, of whom 146.3 million were employed. Employment related to all forms of insurance totaled 2.3 million. Mean annual earnings for full-time civilian workers in June of 2006 were $41,231; median earnings were $33,634)

REVIEW OF LITERATURE

The concept of health insurance was proposed in 1694 by Hugh the Elder Chamberlin from the Peter Chamberlin family. In the late 19th century, "accident insurance" began to be available, which operated much like modern *disability* insurance. This payment model continued until the start of the 20th century in some jurisdictions (like California), where all laws regulating health insurance actually referred to disability insurance. Accident insurance was first offered in the United States by the Franklin Health Assurance Company of Massachusetts. This firm, founded in 1850, offered insurance against injuries arising from railroad and steamboat accidents. Sixty organizations were offering accident insurance in the US by 1866, but the industry consolidated rapidly soon thereafter. While there were earlier experiments, the origins of sickness coverage in the US effectively date from 1890. The first employer-sponsored group disability policy was issued in 1911.

Before the development of medical expense insurance, patients were expected to pay all other health care costs out of their own pockets, under what is known as the fee-for-service business model. During the middle to late 20th century, traditional disability insurance evolved into modern health insurance programs. Today, most comprehensive private health insurance programs cover the cost of routine, preventive, and emergency health care procedures, and also most prescription drugs, but this was not always the case.

Hospital and medical expense policies were introduced during the first half of the 20th century. During the 1920s, individual hospitals began offering services to individuals on a pre-paid basis, eventually leading to the development of Blue Cross organizations. The predecessors of today's Health Maintenance Organizations (HMOs) originated beginning in 1929, through the 1930s and on   during   World   War   II.

A Health insurance policy is a contract between an insurance company and an individual. The contract can be renewable annually or monthly. The type and amount of health care costs that will be covered by the health plan are specified in advance, in the member contract or Evidence of Coverage booklet. The individual policy-holder's payment obligations may take several forms

- **Premium:** The amount the policy-holder pays to the health plan each month to purchase health coverage.

- **Deductible:** The amount that the policy-holder must pay out-of-pocket before the health plan pays its share. For example, a policy-holder might have to pay a $500 deductible per year, before any of their health care is covered by the health plan. It may take several doctor's visits or prescription refills before the policy-holder reaches the deductible and the health plan starts to pay for care.

- **Copayment:** The amount that the policy-holder must pay out of pocket before the health plan pays for a particular visit or service. For example, a policy-holder might pay a $45 copayment for a doctor's visit, or to obtain a prescription. A copayment must be paid each time a particular service is obtained.

- **Coinsurance:** Instead of paying a fixed amount up front (a copayment), the policy-holder must pay a percentage of the total cost. For example, the member might have to pay 20% of the cost of a surgery, while the health plan pays the other 80%. Because there is no upper limit on coinsurance, the policy-holder can end up owing very little, or a significant amount, depending on the actual costs of the services they obtain.

- **Exclusions:** Not all services are covered. The policy-holder is generally expected to pay the full cost of non-covered services out of their own pocket.

- **Coverage limits:** Some health plans only pay for health care up to a certain dollar amount. The policy-holder may be expected to pay any charges in excess of the health plan's maximum payment for a specific service. In addition, some plans have annual or lifetime coverage maximums. In these cases, the health plan will stop payment when they reach the benefit maximum and the policy-holder must pay all remaining costs.

- **Out-of-pocket maximums:** Similar to coverage limits, except that in this case, the member's payment obligation ends when they reach the out-of-pocket maximum, and the health plan pays all further covered costs. Out-of-pocket maximums can be limited to a specific benefit category (such as prescription drugs) or can apply to all coverage provided during a specific benefit year.

Prescription drug plans are a form of insurance offered through many employer benefit plans in the US, where the patient pays a copayment and the prescription drug insurance pays the rest.

Some health care providers will agree to bill the insurance company if patients are willing to sign an agreement that they will be responsible for the amount that the insurance company doesn't pay, as the insurance company pays according to "reasonable" or "customary" charges, which may be less than the provider's usual fee. Health insurance companies also often have a network of providers who agree to accept the reasonable and customary fee and waive the remainder. It will generally cost the patient less to use an in-network provider.

Health plan vs. health insurance

Historically, HMOs tended to use the term "health plan", while commercial insurance companies used the term "health insurance". A health plan can also refer to a subscription-based medical care arrangement offered through health maintenance organization, HMO, PPO, or POS plan. These plans are similar to pre-paid dental, pre-paid legal and pre-paid vision plans. Pre-paid health plans typically pay for a fixed number of services (for instance, $300 in preventive care, a certain number of days of hospice care or care in a skilled nursing facility, a fixed number of home health visits, a fixed number of spinal manipulation charges, etc.) The services offered are usually at the discretion of a utilization review nurse who is often contracted through the managed care entity providing the subscription health plan. This determination may be made either prior to or after hospital admission (concurrent utilization review).

Inherent problems with insurance

Insurance systems must typically deal with two inherent challenges: adverse selection, which affects any voluntary system, and ex-post moral hazard, which affects any insurance system in which a third party bears major responsibility for payment, whether that is an employer or the government. Some national systems with compulsory insurance utilize systems such as risk equalization and community rating to overcome these inherent problems.

Adverse selection

Insurance companies use the term "adverse selection" to describe the tendency for only those who will benefit from insurance to buy it. Specifically when talking about health insurance, unhealthy people are more likely to purchase health insurance because they anticipate large medical bills. On the other side, people who consider themselves to be reasonably healthy may decide that medical insurance is an unnecessary expense; if they see the doctor once a year and it costs $250, that's much better than making monthly insurance payments of $40.

The fundamental concept of insurance is that it balances costs across a large, random sample of individuals (see risk pool). For instance, an insurance company has a pool of 1000 randomly selected subscribers, each paying $100 per month. One person becomes very ill while the others stay healthy, allowing the insurance company to use the money paid by the healthy people to pay for the treatment costs of the sick person. However, when the pool is self-selecting rather than random, as is the case with individuals seeking to purchase health insurance directly, adverse selection is a greater concern. A disproportionate share of health care spending is attributable to individuals with high health care costs. In the US the 1% of the population with the highest spending accounted for 27% of aggregate health care spending in 1996. The highest-spending 5% of the population accounted for more than half of all spending. These patterns were stable through the 1970s and 1980s, and some data suggest that they may have been typical of the mid-to-early 20th century as well. A few individuals have extremely high medical expenses, in extreme cases totaling a half million dollars or more. Adverse selection could leave an insurance company with primarily sick subscribers and no way to balance out the cost of their medical expenses with a large number of healthy subscribers.

Because of adverse selection, insurance companies employ medical underwriting, using a patient's medical history to screen out those whose pre-existing medical conditions pose too great a risk for the risk pool. Before buying health insurance, a person typically fills out a comprehensive medical history form that asks whether the person smokes, how much the person weighs, whether the person has been treated for any of a long list of diseases and so on. In general, those who present large financial burdens are denied coverage or charged high premiums to compensate. One large US industry survey found that roughly 13 percent of applicants for comprehensive, individually purchased health insurance who went through the medical underwriting in 2004 were denied coverage. Declination rates increased significantly with age, rising from 5 percent for individuals 18 and under to just under a third for individuals aged 60 to 64. Among those who were offered coverage, the study found that 76% received offers at standard premium rates, and 22% were offered higher rates. On the other side, applicants can get discounts if they do not smoke and are healthy.

Moral hazard

Moral hazard occurs when an insurer and a consumer enter into a contract under symmetric information, but one party takes action, not taken into account in the contract, which changes the value of the insurance. A common example of moral hazard is third-party payment—when the parties involved in making a decision are not responsible for bearing costs arising from the decision. An example is where doctors and insured patients agree to extra tests which may or may not be necessary. Doctors benefit by avoiding possible malpractice suits, and patients benefit by gaining increased certainty of their medical condition. The cost of these extra tests is borne by the insurance company, which may have had little say in the decision. Co-payments, deductibles, and less generous insurance for services with more elastic demand attempt to combat moral hazard, as they hold the consumer responsible.

Other factors affecting insurance prices

A recent study by Price Waterhouse Coopers examining the drivers of rising health care costs in the US pointed to increased utilization created by increased consumer demand, new treatments, and more intensive diagnostic testing, as the most significant driver. People in developed countries are living longer. The population of those countries is aging, and a larger group of senior citizens requires more intensive medical care than a young healthier population. Advances in medicine and medical technology can also increase the cost of medical treatment. Lifestyle-related factors can increase utilization and therefore insurance prices, such as: increases in obesity caused by insufficient exercise and unhealthy food choices; excessive alcohol use, smoking, and use of street drugs. Other factors noted by the PWC study included the movement to broader-access plans, higher-priced technologies, and cost-shifting from Medicaid and the uninsured to private payers.

CASHLESS HOSPITALIZATION FACILITY

Today, most Health Insurance policies do offer cashless hospitalization facility and route your policy through a Third party Administrator (TPA). However you should be familiar with the terms- Network Hospital and Non-network Hospital. Network Hospitals are those hospitals that your TPA has an agreement with. In case of hospitalization, if you get admitted to a Network Hospital you will be eligible for cashless hospitalization, subject to the other terms and conditions mentioned in your policy being fulfilled. In case you are admitted to a Non-network Hospital, you will have to settle the bills directly to the hospital and then seek re-imbursement through your TPA.

Cashless hospitalization does it mean treatment free of cost?

First, you need to be clear that there is no free treatment. It is just that, in the case of a cashless hospitalization, the insurance company will bear the cost of treatment either fully or partially on your behalf.

Cashless hospitalization is a facility provided by most health insurance policies and enables an insured customer to obtain admission and undergo the required treatment without a direct payment. The assigned TPA will mediate between the healthcare service provider (hospital) and the insurance company and settle the bills on behalf of the insured customer.

However it is important to understand the role of a hospital in cashless hospitalization. The hospital is only a facilitator and has no authority to approve or disapprove any request for cashless hospitalization. Certain protocols laid down by the Insurance Regulatory and Development Authority (IRDA) with respect to cashless hospitalization will need to be adhered to strictly.

Availing the facility of cashless hospitalization

Hospitalization happens under two circumstances – Planned and Emergency. Pre-authorization of the estimated hospital expense is a must to avail this facility.

Planned Hospitalization:

In the case of a planned admission, you would have first consulted a doctor who in turn would have advised you on the probable date of hospitalization. In such a case, you must have applied for an approval of the estimated hospital expenses directly with your TPA at least 4-5 days prior to the date of hospitalization.

In case you have not applied for a pre-authorization sufficiently in advance or if the doctor treating you advises you to get hospitalized immediately after the consultation, Corporate Help Desk will assist you through the pre-authorization procedure. However, you will need to bear in mind that the Corporate Help Desk is only a facilitator and can in no way influence the decision on the approval. The approval can be turned down.

The pre-authorization procedure is detailed below:

Step 1: Establish contact with the Corporate Help Desk at the Hospital

Step 2: At the Corporate Help Desk, you need to present the original health Insurance card issued to you by your TPA

Step 3: Collect the pre-authorization will forms pertaining to your TPA

Step 4: Your pre-authorization will have two sections-

i. General details on the health Insurance policy – to be filled in by you (the Corporate desk will assist you in case you have any difficulty)

ii. Pertains to the treatment recommended for you-needs to be filled in and duly signed by the Doctor who is treating you (do not attempt to fill this section, contact the Corporate desk in case of any difficulty)

Step 5: Return the completed form to the Corporate Help Desk. The personnel at the desk will verify the form for its completeness and let you know in case of any discrepancy

Step 6: Once the form is complete in all respects, the Corporate Help Desk will fax the form to the office of your TPA.

Step 7: The Corporate Help Desk will revert to you on the approval status

Emergency Hospitalization: In case of emergency hospitalization, the corporate help desk will take up your case on a fast track basis with your TPA and is likely to receive approval during any working day.

For cashless treatment it is mandatory for the hospital to have an approval from your TPA. Incase of delay in receiving the approval or when you cannot wait for receiving the approval owing to medical urgency you can undertake the treatment by paying the necessary cash deposit.

If you receive approval from your TPA after paying the cash deposit, you are entitled for refund of the cash deposit.

Cashless facility denial

Cashless hospitalization is linked to the approval of the estimated expenditure on your proposed treatment. In case you do not get your approval you will need to bear the entire expenditure incurred on the treatment. Therefore it is always prudent to get the approval and then get yourself admitted. You could explain the benefits of getting the approval before the date of your admission to your treating doctor as well when he recommends an immediate admission.

Reasons for cashless facility denial

Normally your request for approval might be rejected when:

i. Information contained in the pre-authorization form is insufficient for the TPA to arrive at a decision and further information is not available for various reasons. However the chances of rejection under this criterion are rare since the Corporate Help Desk at the hospital is experienced in complying with pre-authorization formalities and will advise you suitably

ii. The ailment for which hospitalization is being sought by you is not covered under your insurance policy for reasons like pre-existing ailment, specific exclusions (accident admission under the influence of alcohol)

iii. You have exhausted your eligible Medical Insurance cover for the year.

If the actual medical expenses overshoot the pre-approved amount

In case your hospitalization expenses exceed the pre-approved amount, you can approach the Corporate Help Desk to apply for an enhancement of the pre-approved amount.

The Corporate Help Desk will apply for an enhancement on your behalf with the TPA and provide the necessary documentation. In case you have not exhausted your medical insurance limit, it is most likely that your TPA will approve the application for the enhancement – either for the requested enhanced amount or up to your insured limit after deducting the value already utilized by you during the year – whichever is less. If the TPA turns down the request for enhancement you will need to pay the amount incurred in excess of your approved amount directly to the hospital before the discharge

Cashless hospitalization cover

For complete details on the medical expenses that are covered, and those that are not covered, you need to go through your health insurance policy. However, in general, the expenses listed below are not reimbursable under cashless hospitalization

- Registration / Admission Fee

- Telephone Charges

- Visitors / Attenders Charges

- Charges for Diet, which is not part of the administered treatment

- Document Charges

- Toiletries

- Non-medical Expenses

These need to be settled by you directly to the hospital at the time of discharge

STAKEHOLDERS IN HEALTH INSURANCE SECTOR

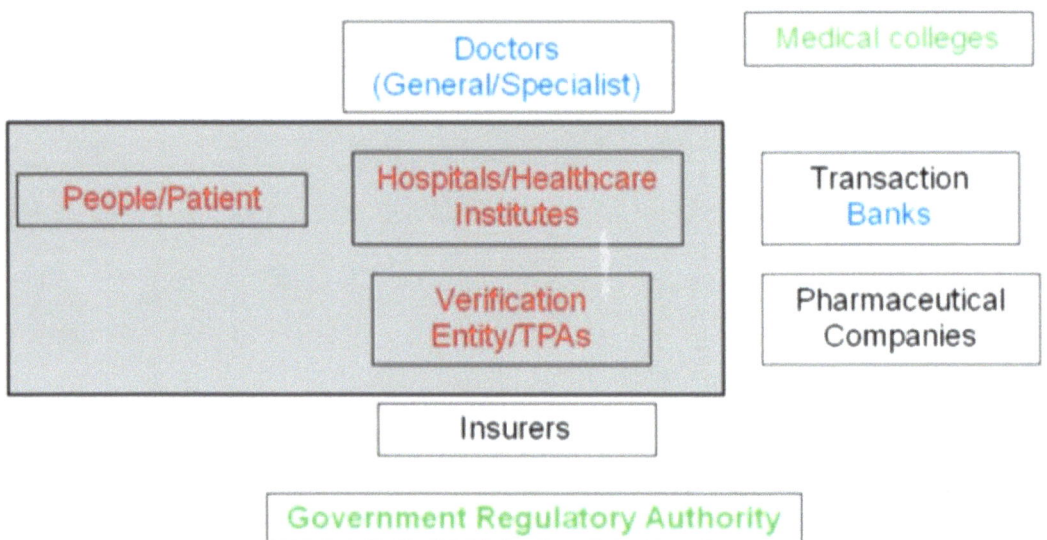

IRDA: Insurance Regulatory & Development Authority, a body constituted under the Ministry of Finance to deal with licensing, regulating and monitoring all activities relating to the insurers, brokers, agents, corporate agents and the TPA's.

TPA: Third party administrators are the new breed of intermediaries in the sector, introduction of whom will benefit both the insured and the insurer. While the insured is benefited by better service, insurers are benefited by reduction in their administrative costs.

Insurers can now outsource their administrative activities, including settlement of claims, to Third party administrators, who offer such services at a cost. It may be noted that TPAs are remunerated by the insurers and so policy holders should welcome such a move since they receive enhanced facilities at no extra cost. Once the policy has been issued, all the records will be passed on to the TPA and all the correspondence of the insured will be with the TPA.

And they will have full-time medical practitioners under their employment who will immediately take a decision on whether the ailment is covered under the policy. TPA license can be granted to any company registered under the companies Act 1956. IRDA, which licenses and regulates these TPAs, has specified stiff entry norms some of which include a minimum capital requirement of 1 Crore, capping the foreign equity at 26% etc.

Partial List of TPAs of India

- TTK HEALTH CARE SERVICES PVT LTD

- MEDI ASSIST INDIA PVT.LTD

- BAJAJ ALLIANZ GENERAL INSURANCE CO LTD.

- E-MEDITEK SOLUTIONS LIMITED

- FAMILY HEALTH PLAN LIMITED

- MEDICARE TPA SERVICES INDIA PVT LTD

- PARAMOUNT HEALTH SERVICES PVT LTD

- UNITED HEALTHCARE INDIA PVT LTD

- GENINS INDIA LTD

- MEDSAVE

- RAKSHA TPA

- M D INDIA

- VIPUL MED CORP

- ALANKIT

- DEDICATED HEALTHCARE SERVICES

- ACCIDENT RELIEF CARE

- GOOD HEALTH PLAN LTD

Insurance Companies

In insurance company, buyers are willing to pay premium to an insurance company that pools people with similar risks and insures them for health expenses. The key distinction is that the premiums are set at a level, which provides a profit to third party and provider institutions. Premiums are based on an assessment of the risk status of the consumer (or of the group of employees) and the level of benefits provided, rather than as a proportion of the consumer's income

Partial List of Insurance Companies of India

Govt Sector

1. Oriental Insurance Company

2. National Insurance Company

3. New India Assurance Company

4. United India Insurance Company

Private Sector

1. ICICI Lombard & ICICI Prudential

2. Max Bupa

3. HDFC ERGO

4. Cholamandalam

5. Bajaj Allianz

6. Reliance Health

7. Royal Sundaram

8. Apollo Munich

Providers (Hospitals)

A hospital is an institution for health care providing treatment by specialized staff and equipment, and often but not always providing for longer- term patient stays. Hospitals are largely staffed by professional physicians, surgeons and nurses.

HEALTH INSURANCE FRAUDS

Health insurance, which accounted for just 2% of the industry's premium income in 2002-03, contributed 21% of the total premium collected by general insurance companies in 2008-09, according to the latest figures available with the Insurance Regulatory Development Authority. It is second only to motor insurance.

Health insurance industry is growing and being chanted about like the new mantra, but, still India is facing a huge loss in this sector because of the everyday increasing fraud claims. Fraudulent health insurance claim actually is a claim generated to cover or deform information which is designed to provide health care benefits. Frauds can be of many types and committed by insurer or the insured. Let's understand them

Defining Fraud & Abuse

It is a matter of concern that 'insurance fraud' is not defined under the Indian Insurance Act. IRDA recently quoted the definition provided by the International Association of Insurance Supervisors (IAIS) which defines fraud as "an act or omission intended to gain dishonest or unlawful advantage for a party committing the fraud or for other related parties."

Other instruments within the Indian legal system, such as the Indian Penal Code (IPC) or Indian Contract Act, also do not offer specific laws. Sections of the IPC which deal with issues of fraudulent act, forgery, cheating etc. are sometimes applied but none of them are specifically targeted at insurance fraud and are inadequate for purpose of acting as an effective deterrent. In absence of specific laws and harsh punishments, prosecution will rarely be successful and if successful, the penalty inadequate to deter others. As social health insurance grows the central and state governments will become one of the largest victims of health insurance fraud and that may be the catalyst that leads to the development of a comprehensive legal framework to tackle health insurance fraud.

In simple parlance, insurance fraud can be defined as: The act of making a statement known to be false and used to induce another party to issue a contract or pay a claim. This act must be wilful and deliberate, involve financial gain, done under false pretences and is illegal.

Healthcare fraud as defined by the National Health Care Anti-Fraud Association (USA): "The deliberate submittal of false claims to private health insurance plans and/or tax-funded public health insurance programs." "Intentional deception or misrepresentation that the individual or entity makes, knowing that the misrepresentation could result in some unauthorized benefit to the individual, or the entity, or to another party."

Abuse can be defined as practices that are inconsistent with business ethics or medical practices and result in an unnecessary cost to claims.

The billing of services that may not be fraudulent, but may be of marginal utility, are inconsistent with acceptable business and/or medical practices, and are intended for the financial gain of a particular individual or corporate can be classified as abuse. Few examples of common health insurance abuse would be - excessive diagnostic tests, extended LoS, conversion of day procedure to overnight admission, admission limited to diagnostic investigations etc.

Fraud is willful and deliberate, involves financial gain, done under false pretense and is illegal. Abuse generally fails to meet one or more of these criteria, hence the subtle difference. Needless to say that the main purpose of both fraud and abuse is financial gain.

TYPES OF HEALTH INSURANCE FRAUDS

Health insurance frauds can be classified broadly into following typs:-

Deliberate and Opportunity Fraud

Deliberate fraud is purposeful act of presenting accident or loss which is covered under the policy. Whereas, opportunity fraud is created by a policyholders by over stressing a genuine claim or providing wrong information related to the pre-existing diseases etc. to get the underwriting done in their favor.

External and Internal Fraud

External fraud is claimed by either an individual or entities like policyholder, beneficiaries, medical service providers or vendors against a company. Internal fraud on the other hand is carried out against a policyholder or its company by other employees like manager, executive or agents.

Policyholder's Fraud

Now-a-days, consumers have become aware of the norms, features and rules of the insurance and have started getting benefited by being involved in frauds. Policyholder frauds are divided into 3 categories – eligibility fraud, claim fraud and application fraud.

Eligibility Fraud

This fraud generally constitutes the falsification of the information provided about the insured's employment status, pre-existing diseases or information concerning the dependent. Here, the beneficiary is paid benefits illicitly, for example, if a person submits claim for the dependent or relative who is not covered under the policy. Another case is when a part-time employee is not covered under some health plan provided by the company for full-time employees but, my generating false records with any HR employee he is successful in receiving the benefits.

Application Fraud

It is generally committed in the health insurance sector where the consumer knowingly enters forged information in its application related to the pre-existing diseases, claim or important dates. For instance, a policyholder might not enter the details related to his pre-existing diseases or serious medical conditions in order to get an extensive cover and have problem free claim filing. Even, at times, the employer plays with the joining date of the employee by getting things approved from the insurance company.

Claim Fraud

When a consumer enters an illegal claim for whose benefit he is not entitled for, the fraud is called claim fraud. He can ask for a false claim which is especially seen under maternity covers. In such intentional cases, the provider and member are seen to go for collusion and thus, benefiting the physician. These kinds of groups are also known as fraud rings. Another case - a policyholder can even turn to create an insurance speculation, wherein, he purchases several health insurance policies without letting the insurance companies know this fact and enjoy claim settlement from all.

As relevant to health insurance, the type of fraud committed by customer, intermediary - agent, broker, healthcare provider either individually or jointly or in connivance with internal staff of insurance company/TPA vary in nature and modus operandi.

Commonly committed fraud by a customer of health insurance relate to:

- Covering pre-existing disease (PED) / chronic ailment, manipulating pre-policy health check-up findings.

- Fake/ fabricated documents to meet policy terms conditions.

- Inflated bills, impersonation.

- Participating in fraud rings, purchasing multiple policies.

- Staged accidents and fake disability claims.

The agents and brokers are usually involved in fraud relating to:

- Providing fake policy to customer and siphoning off premium.

- Manipulating pre-policy health check-up records.

- Guiding customer to hide PED/material fact to obtain cover or to file claim.

- Participating in fraud rings and facilitating policies in fictitious names.

- Channelising customers to rouge providers.

- Fudging data in group health covers.

Due to the absence of standard medical protocols, no oversight of a regulator, the provider induced fraud and abuse in India forms quite a large portion of fraudulent claims. It would be quite difficult for a customer to file a fraudulent claim or fake medical documents without connivance of treating doctor or hospital.

Provider related fraud usually pertain to:

- Overcharging, inflated billing, billing for services not provided.

- Unbundling and up coding.

- Unwarranted procedures, excessive investigations, expensive medicines.

- Over utilization, extended length of stay.

- Fudging records, patient history.

The employees of insurance company / TPA could also be involved in committing fraud by expecting receiving favours / kickbacks, colluding with other fraudsters / fraud rings, siphoning premium etc.

TRIGGERS OF HEALTH INSURANCE FRAUDS

It has been observed that frauds pertaining to health insurance usually possess some sort of common trends or patterns. There are certain parameters that can be employed as a trigger to detect false claims or practices which have been enlisted below:

Policy and claim history related triggers

1. Claims from a policy with only one member at minimum sum insured amount.

2. Multiple claims with repeated hospitalization (under a specific policy at different hospitals or at one hospital of one member of family and different hospitals for other members of family), multiple claims towards the end of policy period, close proximity of claims.

3. Claims made immediately after a policy sum insured enhancement.

4. Claims from a member with history of frequent change of insurer or gap in previous insurance policy.

5. Claims for policy with evidence of significant over/under insurance as compared to insured are income/life-style.

6. Claims from a non-traceable person or where courier/cheque has been returned from insured's documented address.

7. Second claim in the same year for an acute medical illness/surgical minor illness in the same policy period for main claim.

8. Claims from members with no claim free years, i.e. regular claim history.

Provider location related triggers

9. Claims from a hospital located far away from insured's residence.

10. Claims from a hospital already identified on a watch list or black listed hospital.

---

11. Claims on hospital stationary without landline phone number, registration number, pin code or doctor's qualification stated.

12. Claims submitted that cause suspicion due to format or content that looks "too perfect" in order. Pharmacy bills in chronological order or claim documents with color photocopies. Perfect claim file with all criteria fulfilled with no deficiencies.

13. Claims with visible tempering of documents, overwriting in diagnosis/treatment papers, discharge summary, bills etc. same handwriting and flow in all documents from first prescription to admission to discharge. Bills generated on a word document or documents without proper signature, name and stamp.

14. Claims without supporting pre-post hospitalization papers/bills.

15. Claims with apparent discrepancy in diagnosis and line of treatment: irrelevant investigations for a particular ailment, mismatch in ICD and CPT code/procedure description, line of treatment/procedure inconsistent with insured's profile/gender/age or season.

16. Claims with incomplete/poor medical history- complaints/presenting symptoms not mentioned, only line of treatment given, supporting documentation vague or insufficient.

17. Claims without signature of insured.

18. Reimbursement claim from a network hospital.

19. Claims with missing information like post-operative histopathology reports, surgical/anesthetist notes missing in surgical cases.

20. Claims with similar format/pattern/clinical details in discharge card/bill from a particular provider.

Diagnosis or surgery-specific triggers

21. Claims for hospitalization due to chronic/life style diseases management.

22. Claims with LoS far in excess of average LoS for a particular ailment.

23. Claims relating to infertility, abortion, miscarriage etc.

24. Claims for medical management admission for exactly 24 hours to cover OP treatment, expensive investigations.

25. Claims for acute medical illness which are uncommon e.g. encephalitis, cerebral malaria, monkey bite etc.

26. Claims for surgical conditions being treated conservatively.

27. Claims where clinical findings do not correlate with chief complaints or diagnosis or line of treatment; exaggeration of classical clinical findings to portray severity in acute medical illness.

28. Claims with unjustified admission in ICU or use of general anesthesia or assistant surgeon in a minor complexity or mild severity of condition.

Billing and tariff based triggers

29. Claims where the cost of treatment is much higher than expected for underlying etiology.

30. Claims with high relatively proportion of pharmacy costs or physician fees (more than 50% of total claim value).

31. High value claim from a small hospital/nursing home, particularly in class B or C cities not consistent with ailment and/or provider profile.

32. Claims with no intimation of claim till the submission of claim documents, delayed preauthorization request send after second day of hospital admission or extraordinary delay in reporting of claims; claim intimation on weekend or public holidays.

Member based triggers

33. Claims from members creating abnormal pressure to settle claim; unusually high knowledge of policy terms, claim process, medical terminology or eagerness to negotiate claim amount.

34. Claims where member is unwilling to meet face to face or does not provide phone number in the claim form. Claims from member where attitude is evasive, hostile, uncooperative, complaining.

MANAGING FRAUD

A. Process improvements or modifications

In this section, methods of identification, mitigation and management of fraud are considered within the context of process improvements or modifications that can be implemented by the insurer. Possible areas to consider are set out below.

1) **Tele-underwriting or proposal verification call:** This should ideally be a centrally controlled process to ensure that the proposal form contents reflect the policyholder's understanding and specifically including confirmation that no PEDs exist. This should be done after a proposal is received but before a policy is issued. It helps to minimize agent-led fraud and the use of recorded calls may help substantiate evidence of fraud at claims stage. In addition, this call can be utilized to confirm that the policyholder fully understands the benefits and exclusions of the policy.

Cost: low for verification call

Complexity to develop/administer: medium - agent needs to disclose policyholder's contact number

2) **Pre-authorization:** This process is a vital component of the health insurance claims system. It is the first level check to curb fraud and capable of eliminating or reducing the likelihood of its occurrence. However, whether due to an insurer's processes and systems not being robust enough or lack of awareness on the part of customer or provider, this process is often not adhered to in the manner required and the key components of this process which make it effective, need to be implemented properly.

    a. Pre-authorization requests for scheduled surgeries must be submitted at least 24 hours before admission

b. Implementation of the standardized pre-authorization, discharge summary and billing format must be fast-tracked.

3) **Intimation to insurer or TPA:** The first intimation call to the insurer or TPA is a very rich source of information about the status of the policyholder at time of admission. As a result, this intelligence should be used in an optimum manner. The best practice in respect of what information should be sought at the intimation stage to mitigate fraud, should be documented and distributed.

Cost: low

Complexity to develop/administer: low

4) **Explanation of benefits:** In some markets, insurers send the policyholder a detailed breakdown of what benefits they have paid for. This can be very effective way to check if any impersonation or billing for services not provided had occurred.

Cost: low

Complexity to develop/administer: low

5) **Fraud detection tools and technology:** Insurers in advanced markets deploy robust technology and data analytics processes for detecting outlier behavior or for predictive modeling. These function as a kind of early warning system for detecting fraud. The solutions offered can work in conjunction with existing practices to create a robust framework for early detection / prevention of fraud.

Cost: medium

Complexity to develop / administer: medium

6) **Whistleblower policy (company level):** Develop a reporting and rewards system that will motivate individuals to alert an insurer about individual cases of fraud or systematic fraud. This can be a very attractive mechanism through which the general population can be engaged in the fight against fraud. In addition this is a mechanism for disgruntled co-conspirators to exit a risky situation whilst claiming credit for stopping it.

Cost: nil, only based on outcome

Complexity to develop/administer: low

7) **"Name & shame" guidelines: (company level):** Publicly disclosing names of individuals and institutions involved in a confirmed case of health insurance fraud, especially when a criminal or civil case has already been filed is an effective way of raising community awareness that insurance fraud will not be tolerated. An internal media policy about how and what to disclose as well as in which situations, can provide valuable guidance as the time to take such decisions is usually short.

Cost: nil

Complexity to develop/administer: medium, proper legal review of all information released is required to avoid accusations of libel or slander

B. Industry Intervention

As an industry evolves, certain systematic requirements emerge. These are generally intended to organize and structure the industry and are often best implemented by the industry through a collective body, such as General Insurance Council (GIC) or through a less formal forum specifically designed for such tasks. In recent few months, General Insurance Council has taken initiative in fraud data sharing among member companies and has also looked at classification, monitoring and developing templates for data sharing. The data sharing should also lead to collective action for effective deterrence, either through GI Council or the recently constituted Health Insurance Forum.

Key to the success of collective action will be blacklisting / de-empanelment by all of those entities who are proven to indulge in fraud and pursuing punitive action, recovery of money. While data sharing can be the start point, achievable in a short time, the industry level interventions need to be wide and deep for all encompassing impact. Some of the initiatives suggested below are equally easy to achieve if industry would set out the task.

> **Education:** Fraud can happen inadvertently and due to ignorance. It is in the industry's interest to create education and awareness collateral that creates awareness about the impact of insurance fraud and its implications. This can be deployed for all levels of insurance and TPA employees. It can include content for consumer and provider education to create awareness and ensure that individuals are not inadvertently facilitating fraud.

Cost: Low

Complexity to develop/administer: Low

> **Contracting:** In the absence of appropriate law on insurance fraud, the industry should

develop model clauses for incorporation into policy contract, in contract with providers, in agency/broker contracts etc. The definition of what constitutes fraud, what penalties and punitive actions would follow upon confirmation of fraud could be spelt out clearly in the contract and claw back provisions for recovery of money into some of these contracts should be explored.

➢ **Deterrence guidelines:** Industry recommendation on steps and processes an insurer can undertake when fraud is suspected and when it is confirmed. This would provide a common framework or best practice on how to respond. It is to be noted that insurance industry has not made adequate use of Medical Council of India (MCI) guidelines on code of conduct and ethics for medical practitioners. The effective deterrence for medical fraternity can only come from medical regulator, in the absence of which the good offices of MCI can be utilized.

Cost: nil

Complexity to develop / administer: low

➢ **Benchmarks:** The industry could collaborate with IIB to create benchmarks that individual stakeholders can utilize to obtain better insight into their overall performance. A proven approach in this direction is to aggregate all industry data in a single data warehouse and then develop various benchmarks that an individual insurer can compare itself with. Naturally, these benchmarks need to be developed carefully so that the comparison is on a like-for-like basis.

Cost: medium (one time and ongoing)

Complexity to develop/administer: medium

> **Medical protocols and treatment guidelines:** The industry should advocate for the development and dissemination of independent 3rd party evidence based standard medical protocols and treatment guidelines.

> **Provider billing ID and registration portal:** A version of this control mechanism has been very effective in curbing rampant fraud amongst providers of durable medical equipment to Medicare beneficiaries in the US. The General Insurance Council or newly constituted Health Forum should build a provider registration portal.

Cost: low/medium

Complexity to develop/administer: low

> **Watch list creation and maintenance:** All TPAs and insurers maintain and share their own lists of blacklisted providers. A common listing of these entities by collecting this information from all TPAs and insurers would benefit the industry as a shared knowledge repository. The development of such a repository would involve a "one-time" effort to collect existing blacklists from TPAs and insurers and then compile them into user-friendly format and an "on-going" effort to maintain it. Such a watch list would resemble a website with a secure password restricted area which would contain indexed watch lists of individuals and corporate entities which have previously defrauded or abused the insurance system. This would be a centralized resource which insurers and TPA can assess and search and update. The credibility of the data will be enhanced by replacing an ad-hoc sharing of individual lists provided between insurers.

Cost: low

Complexity to develop/administer: low/medium

➤ **Fraud investigator training program:** A structured training program along with mandatory examination, as well as continuing education requirements should be developed for fraud investigators. All fraud investigators must meet a minimum skill set requirement. In addition, there should be a mechanism whereby a fraud investigator can be assessed and certified for higher skill levels. This would create a cadre of professional and highly skilled fraud investigators. It may be desirable to ensure that these investigators are licensed by the IRDA.

Cost: low

Complexity to develop/administer: low/medium

➤ **Whistleblower system & rewards:** (industry level): In case of actionable information about larger and more systematic fraud cases which span across entities, the industry (through IRDA or GIC or the newly formed Health Insurance Forum) may wish to coordinate a reward program. Modalities of reward programs initiated by insurers as well as other government entities, such as tax or customs departments, might need to be studied.

Cost: nil, only based on outcome

Complexity to develop/administer: medium

> - **Capacity and awareness development in police and prosecution agencies:** In conjunction with building a cadre of fraud investigators, the industry will need to invest resources in training police and public prosecutors. Police officers are not familiar with intricacies of insurance processes and that can hinder progress in fraud investigations. Similarly, public prosecutors need requisite insurance knowledge to effectively prosecute offenders. A training program for police economic offence investigators and prosecutors could be conducted by the same entity tasked with training fraud investigators.

C. **Government or Regulatory Interventions**

> - **Regulatory action against licensed bodies:** IRDA's jurisdiction spans insurers, agents, brokers and TPAs. While these entities are governed by detailed guidelines, regulations and are subjected to regular inspections/audits by Regulator, the action and penalty upon confirmation of connivance or active involvement in fraudulent activity should also be clearly spent out, leading to suspension/revocation of license. Unfortunately there is no equivalent regulator for the supervision of providers, which puts the onus on the Health Forum to take collective action against providers indulging in health insurance fraud. It is also necessary that MCI and Ministry of Health play an active role in bringing fraudulent hospitals and doctors to account. The Health Forum should also make a concerted effort to address these issues with members from the provider space.

- ➤ **Specific laws against insurance fraud:** Many countries have very specific laws against insurance fraud and occasionally more specific laws pertaining to social insurance fraud. The specific laws can contain clauses which ensure speedy resolution of cases, thus enhancing the impact of the law.

- ➤ **Introduction of claw back provisions:** Insurance fraud laws which contain provisions which enable an insurer to recover payments, if fraud is proven subsequently. These have been found to be very effective in other countries. Usually such "claw back" provisions are limited to a certain time period, i.e. 3 or 5 years.

- ➤ **Regulatory requirements for specific anti-fraud units and capabilities in insurers:** The licensing and inspection regulations of various insurance regulators allow them to seek detailed information about an insurer's anti-fraud capabilities. Insurers who do not demonstrate adequate safeguards may be fined. The policy is supposed to lay framework for fraud management department, classification of potential areas of fraud, information sharing mechanism, due diligence etc.

- ➤ **Anti-fraud public messaging:** The regulator and government can collectively undertake public messaging which highlights the impact (higher premiums) and consequences (legal action) of insurance fraud. Such campaigns are generally planned as ongoing initiatives which are further enforced by "name & shame" initiatives. IRDA has run number of campaigns on policy holder education, insurance literacy.

INDIAN PENAL SYSTEM CODE (IPC) AND INDIAN CONTRACT ACT SECTIONS RELEVANT IN HEALTH INSURANCE

➤ Section 25: A person is said to act fraudulently if he acts with the intent to defraud but not otherwise.

➤ Section 191: Giving false document "Whoever, being legally bound by an oath or by an express provision of law to state the truth, or being bound by law to make a declaration upon any subject, makes any statement which is false, and which he either knows or believes to be false or does not believe to be true, is said to give false evidence". Issuing or signing a false certificate "Whoever issues or signs any certificate required by law to be given or signed, or relating to any fact of which such certificate is by law admissible in evidence, knowing or believing that such certificate is false in any material point, shall be punished in the same manner as if he gave false evidence".

➤ Section 198: Using as true, a certificate that is known to be false "Whoever corruptly uses or attempts to use any such certificate as a true certificate, knowing the same to be false in any material point, shall be punished in the same manner as if he gave false evidence".

➤ Section 199: False statement made in declaration which is by law receivable as evidence "Whoever, in any declaration made or subscribed by him, which declaration any Court of Justice, or any public servant or other person, is bound or authorized by law to receive as evidence of any fact, makes any statement which is false, and which he either knows or believes to be false or does not believe to be true, touching any point material to the object for which the declaration is made or used, shall be punished in the same manner as if he gave false evidence".

➢ Section 205: False personation for purpose of act proceeding in suit or prosecution "Whoever falsely personates another, and in such assumed character makes any admission or statement, or confesses judgment, or causes any process to be issued or becomes bail or security, or does any other act in any suit or criminal prosecution, shall be punished with imprisonment of either description for a term which may extend to three years or with fine, or with both".

➢ Section 415: Whoever, by deceiving any person, fraudulently or dishonestly induces the person so deceived to deliver any property to any person, or to consent that any person shall retain any property, or intentionally induces the person so deceived to do or omit to do anything which he would not do omit if he were not so deceived, and which act or omission causes or is likely to cause damage or harm to that person in body, mind, reputation or property, is said to "cheat".

➢ Section 463: Relates to forgery. "Whoever makes any false documents or false electronic record or part of a document or electronic record, with intent to cause damage or injury, to the public or to any person, or to support any claim or title, or to cause any person to part with property, or to enter into any express or implied contract, or with intent to commit fraud or that fraud may be committed, commits forgery."

➢ Section 464: Making a false document

  • A person is said to make a false document or false electronic record who dishonestly or fraudulently (a) makes, signs, seals or executes a document or part of a document; (b) makes or transmits any electronic record or part of any electronic record; (c) affixes any digital signature on any electronic record; (d) makes any mark denoting the execution of a document or the authenticity of the digital signature.

- With the intention of causing it to be believed that such document or part of document, electronic record or digital signature was made, signed, sealed, executed, transmitted or affixed by or by the authority of a person by whom or by whose authority he knows that it was not made, signed, sealed, executed or affixed.

➤ Section 468: Forgery for the purpose of cheating. "Whoever commits forgery, intending that the document or Electronic Record forged shall be used for the purpose of cheating, shall be punished with imprisonment of either description for a term which may extend to seven years, and shall also be liable to fine".

➤ Section 471: Using as genuine, a forged document or electronic data. "Whoever fraudulently or dishonestly uses as genuine any document or electronic record which he knows or has reason to believe to be a forged document or electronic record, shall be punished in the same manner as if he had forged such document or electronic record".

➤ Section 477 A: Relates to falsification of accounts. This may be an applicable section in some cases of health insurance fraud. "Whoever, being a clerk, officer or servant or employed or acting in capacity of a clerk, officer or servant, wilfully and with intent to defraud, destroys, alters, mutilates or falsifies any book, electronic record, paper, writing, valuable security or account which belongs to or is in the possession of his employer or has been received by him for on behalf of his employer or wilfully, and with intent to defraud, makes or abets the making of any false entry in, or omits or alters or abets the omission or alteration of any material particular from or in, any such book, electronic record, paper, writing, valuable security or account, shall be punished with imprisonment of either description for a term which may extend to seven years, or with fine, or with both."

> Applicability of Section 17 in The Indian Contract Act, 1872

"Fraud" means and includes any of the following acts committed by a party to a contract, or with his connivance, or by his agent, with intent to deceive another party thereto of his agent, or to induce him to enter into the contract:-

☐ The suggestion, as a fact, of that which is not true, by one who does not believe it to be true (across entities)

☐ The active concealment of a fact by one having knowledge or belief of the fact (across entities)

☐ A promise made without any intention of performing it (intermediary/ sales staff)

☐ Any other act fitted to deceive (across entities)

Laws Applicable in USA

In the US, health insurance fraud can be prosecuted under federal laws or state laws. The Health Insurance Portability and Accountability Act of 1996 (HIPAA) makes health care fraud a federal crime. Health care fraud occurs when anyone knowingly and willfully executes, or attempts to execute, a scheme to defraud any health care benefit program in connection with the delivery of or payment for health care benefits, or obtains any property of the health care benefit program by false representations. A person who violates the statute may be fined, imprisoned up to 10 years, or both. If the fraud results in injury to a patient, he may be imprisoned up to 20 years. If death results, he may be imprisoned for life (18 U.S.C. § 1347). The statute applies to fraud against private insurance companies and government health care programs. It also applies to any insurance program involving medical payments (e.g. health insurance, automobile insurance, workers' compensation) (18 U.S.C. § 24).

HIPAA also prohibits knowingly and willfully falsifying, concealing, or covering up a material fact; or making a false statement; or using or making any false or fraudulent document in connection with the delivery of or payment for health care benefits or services. A person who violates this law may be fined, imprisoned up to five years, or both (47 U.S.C. § 1035).

False Claims

A person who knowingly presents a fraudulent claim to the U.S. government (e.g. Medicare) is fined between $5,000 and $10,000 plus treble damages (three times the government's losses) under the federal False Claims Act (31 U.S.C. § 3729).

False Statements

A person who knowingly and willfully falsifies, conceals, or covers up a material fact; makes a false statement; or uses or makes a false or fraudulent statement to a government agency is fined, imprisoned up to five years, or both under the federal False Statements to a Government Agency law (18 U.S.C. § 1001).

Mail Fraud

A person who engages in a scheme to defraud any person that involves the use of the U.S. mail may be fined, imprisoned up to 20 years, or both. If the attempt to defraud affects a financial institution (e.g. bank or credit union), the person may be fined up to $1,000,000, imprisoned up to 30 years, or both (18 U.S.C. § 1341). Mailing a fraudulent claim violates this statute.

Wire Fraud

A person who uses an interstate wire transmission (e.g. telephone, automated claim system) to carry out a fraudulent scheme may be fined, imprisoned up to 20 years, or both. If the attempt to defraud affects a financial institution (e.g., bank or credit union), the person may be fined up to $1,000,000, imprisoned up to 30 years, or both (18 U.S.C. § 1343).

Racketeer Influenced and Corrupt Organization Act (RICO)

Under RICO, criminal charges and civil lawsuits can be brought against a person engaged in a "pattern of racketeering activity." Racketeering activity includes mail or wire fraud. Submitting a number of fraudulent insurance claims over a period of time would constitute a "pattern" of racketeering.

Criminal penalties include a fine, imprisonment up to 20 years (or more in certain circumstances), or both and forfeiture of any proceeds gained from the racketeering activity (18 U.S.C. § 1693). Civil remedies include treble damages, meaning an insurer could collect punitive damages equal to three times their actual losses, and reasonable attorney fees (18 U.S.C. § 1964).

The applicable state laws are:

Most states have statutes regarding fraud and some specifically address insurance fraud. Insurance fraud statutes generally define what constitutes fraud and what penalties or damages may be imposed. Both the National Conference of Insurance Legislators (NCOIL) and the National Association of Insurance Commissioners (NAIC) have insurance fraud model acts.

NCOIL's model act includes criminal penalties, restitution, administrative penalties, and civil remedies for insurance fraud. NAIC's model requires fraud warnings on insurance applications and claim forms, fraud reporting by insurers, the creation of fraud units within insurance departments, insurer anti-fraud initiatives, and penalties.

Usually the States define insurance fraud as a class D felony. For example, in Connecticut, a person is guilty of insurance fraud when, with the intent to injure, defraud, or deceive any insurance company, he knowingly presents false, incomplete, or misleading information in support of an insurance application, claim, or other benefit. This subjects a person to a fine up to $5,000, up to five years imprisonment, or both (C.G.S. § 53a-215).

PROTOCOLS FOR DIFFERENT LEVELS OF MISCONDUCT/FRAUD

1. Customer- occasionally the customer is the perpetrator of the fraud. Customer frauds are generally soft in nature, unless the customer is a professional claimant who regularly submits false claims.

(a)   Misconduct - False or suppressed history at proposal stage to hide PED and secure coverage.

        Action 1 - Policy cancellation for hiding material fact, without refund of premium

        Action 2 - Sharing info to industry to blacklist customer at common database

(b)   Misconduct - Managing medical reports at proposal stage for gaining cover or reducing premium.

        Action 1 - Policy cancellation for hiding material fact, without refund of premium

        Action 2 - Sharing info to industry to blacklist customer at common database

(c)   Misconduct - Inflating bills manually for genuine treatment.

        Action 1 - Policy cancellation for hiding intentional misrepresentation, without refund of premium

        Action 2 - Sharing information with industry blacklist

        Action 3 - Add to name and shame list

        Action 4 - Legal remedy, such as FIR on insured

(d)   Misconduct - Manipulating ailment for seeking coverage not entitled to, for example an excluded ailment is masked as legitimate claim (undergoing hernia in 1st two years of exclusion phase and claiming as acute abdomen or appendectomy).

        Action 1 - Policy cancellation for hiding intentional misrepresentation, without refund of premium

Action 2 - Sharing information with industry blacklist

Action 3 - Add to name and shame list

(e) Misconduct - Getting non beneficiary treated under the policy and claimed for self by customer.

Action 1 - Policy cancellation for hiding intentional misrepresentation, without refund of premium

Action 2 - Sharing information with industry blacklist

Action 3 - Add to name and shame list

Action 4 - Legal remedy, such as FIR on both doctor and insured

(f) Misconduct - Colluding with provider (hospital) for converting OP to IP claim.

Action 1 - Policy cancellation for hiding intentional misrepresentation, without refund of premium

Action 2 - Sharing information with industry blacklist

Action 3 - Add too name and shame list

Action 4 - Legal remedy, such as FIR on both doctor and insured

(g) Misconduct - Colluding with provider for fake claim documentation.

Action 1 - Policy cancellation for hiding intentional misrepresentation, without refund of premium

Action 2 - Sharing information with industry blacklist

Action 3 - Add to name and shame list

Action 4 - Legal remedy, such as FIR on both doctor and insured

(h) Misconduct - Fake PTD claim.

Action 1 - Policy cancellation for hiding intentional misrepresentation, without refund of premium

Action 2 - Delist from future PA coverage eligibility

Action 3 - Add to name and shame list

Action 4 - Legal remedy, such as FIR on both doctor and insured

(i)   Misconduct - Manipulated death claim by claimant.

Action 1- Policy cancellation for hiding intentional misrepresentation, without refund of premium.

Action 2 - Delist from future PA coverage eligibility

Action 3 - Add to name and shame list

Action 4 - Legal remedy, such as FIR on both doctor and insured

2. Provider - Empanelled network provider are have different fraud patterns than non-network hospitals. Whereas the non-network hospitals do not directly receive payments from hospitals and they may help a policy holder in lodging a false claim, the empanelled providers are direct recipients of claimed amount thus the fraud they indulge in is different.

(a)   Misconduct - Inflation in claim cost by various methods

(i) Misconduct - Substituting low cost medicine with high cost brands

Action 1 - Warning with temporary suspension for 3 months from network

Action 2 - Pan-industry suspension

(ii) Misconduct - Getting unnecessary/ unwanted tests done

Action 1 - Warning with temporary suspension for 3 months from network

Action 2 - Pan-industry suspension

(iii) Misconduct - Billing extra number of physician visits

Action 1 - Warning with temporary suspension for 3 months from network

Action 2 - Pan-industry suspension

(iv) Misconduct - Unbundling of procedures and billing them separately

Action 1 - Warning with temporary suspension for 3 months from network

Action 2 - Pan-industry suspension

(v) Misconduct - Increase in length of stay, either pre or post admission, without the knowledge of the customer

Action 1 - Warning with temporary suspension for 3 months from network

(vi) Misconduct - Upgrading the accommodation category

Action 1 - Warning with temporary suspension for 3 months from network

Action 2 - Pan-industry suspension

(b)   Misconduct - Hiding PED ailment

Action 1 - Warning with temporary suspension for 1yr from network

Action 2 - Pan-industry suspension

(c)   Misconduct - Lodging fake claim without customer knowledge based on previous card details

Action 1 - Permanent de-empanelment

Action 2 - Pan-industry blacklisting

Action 3 - Add to name and shame list

Action 4 - Legal remedy, such as FIR on provider

(d)   Misconduct - Colluding with agent or corporate group to have a set of insured for lodging fake claims.

     Action 1 - Permanent de-empanelment

     Action 2 - Pan-industry blacklisting

     Action 3 - Add to name and shame list

     Action 4 - Legal remedy, such as FIR on provider

(e)   Misconduct - Offering free OPD to customers with insurance cards and later lodging fake claims on their behalf.

     Action 1 - Permanent de-empanelment

     Action 2 - Pan-industry blacklisting

     Action 3 - Add to name and shame list

     Action 4 - Legal remedy, such as FIR on provider

3. Agent - Are a unique link between customer and insurer and hence can defraud both customer and insurer.

(a)   Misconduct - Provide fake policy to the customer and siphoning off the premium amount.

     Action 1 - License cancellation

     Action 2 - Across industry blacklisting

     Action 3 - Add to name and shame list

     Action 4 - Legal remedy, such as FIR on agent

(b)   Misconduct - Guiding customer to hide PED for getting policy issued.

     Action 1 - Warning with temporary suspension for 6 months from industry business

     Action 2 - Pan-industry suspension

     Action 3 - Add to name and shame list

(c)   Misconduct - Being part of fraud ring can facilitate policies on fictitious name and address.

Action 1 - License cancellation

Action 2 - Pan-industry blacklisting

Action 3 - Add to name and shame list

Action 4 - Legal remedy, such as FIR on agent

(d)   Misconduct - Facilitate customers to rouge providers for facilitating fraud claims on share basis.

Action 1 - License cancellation

Action 2 - Pan-industry blacklisting

Action 3 - Add to name and shame list

Action 4 - Legal remedy, such as FIR on agent

CONCLUSION

Although insurance emerged in our country more than a century ago, there is still little awareness about insurance, its advantages, product details etc. The situation is worse in respect of health insurance. In recent years, after the industry was opened up, there seems to be better awareness about health insurance and products. The awareness campaigns led by IRDA and entry of Third-Party Administrators and brokers have also helped in creating awareness about health insurance products and their benefits.

For instance, with regard to coverage for dental care, the coverage gives a favourable reimbursement for individuals who have gone for routine dental care checkups and treatment. The routine checkups though are taken to be a palliative measure to prevent serious future complications, the overindulgence of the insured results in augmented financial participation causing overuse of basic service or the most expensive procedures.

The worst things of all, some of the procedures undergone may ignore the purpose of coverage, and may also include procedures, which are purely for cosmetic enhancement. Therefore, it is necessary that while providing health insurance coverage, it is mandatory to control the activities of health care service providers and their beneficiaries- the purchasers of insurance. The interactions between them are purely subjective and therefore open up avenues for indulging in unwarranted gains (fraud). Health care professionals and institutions being on a higher plane or status than the patient allow the health provider to be in a better position to influence the insured. Such indulgence prevents insurance business from surviving to meet the needs of an insured with a real need of health insurance to pay for an emergency health care service.

The Law of Contract defines Fraud (under section 17 of the Act) as "The active concealment of a fact by one having knowledge or belief of the fact". It also states that the mere silence of the facts likely to affect the willingness of a person to enter into contract is not fraud, unless the circumstances of the case are such that, regard being had to them, it is the duty of the person keeping silence to speak, or unless his silence is, in itself, equivalent to a speech. Therefore, for avoiding fraud insurers ought to work closer with other insurers, brokers, police, etc, in getting access to information about their potential customers. In UK, the ABI does an excellent job of liaising with the police and other organizations on behalf of the insurance industry. It is very effective at transferring information to insurance companies, and acting as a focal point for information.

Health insurers should understand that quality underwriting is the sine qua non for the development of a healthy insurance business. Indian insurers need to regain control of their health business, which is one of the fastest-growing segments in the market .They need to commit resources not merely to develop the health insurance portfolio but also the detection of frauds.

ATTRIBUTES OF AN INVESTIGATOR

- Inquisitive
- Observant
- Focused
- Open minded
- Curious
- Perseverant
- Persistent
- Good Mannered
- Good Listening Skills
- Unbiased mind
- Unprejudiced mind
- Ability to play role
- Ability to put people at ease
- Ability to obtain other's cooperation
- Ability to reach a logical conclusion

ANNEXURE: IRDA GUIDELINES ON FRAUD

Fraud Detection, Classification, Monitoring and Reporting by Insurers

The Authority has taken a number of measures to address the various risks faced by the insurance companies. Some of these include:

- The Corporate Governance guidelines mandate insurance companies to set up a Risk Management Committee to lay down Risk Management Strategy.

- As part of the Responsibility Statement which forms part of the Management Report filed with the Authority under the IRDA (Preparation of Financial Statements and Auditors' Report of Insurance Companies) Regulations, 2002, Management of the insurance company discloses the adequacy of systems in place to safeguard the assets for preventing and detecting fraud and other irregularities, on an annual basis.

The Guidelines mandate insurance companies to put in place, as part of their corporate governance structure, fraud detection and mitigation measures and submit periodic reports to the Authority in the formats prescribed herein.

1. Anti-Fraud Policy:

All insurance companies are required to have in place the Anti-Fraud Policy duly approved by the Board. The policy shall duly recognize the principle of proportionality and reflect the nature, scale and complexity of the business of specific insurers and risks to which they are exposed. It should consider relevant factors like organizational structure, insurance products offered, technology used, market conditions etc. As fraud can be perpetrated by collusion involving more than one party, insurer should adopt a holistic approach to adequately identify, measure, control and monitor fraud risk and accordingly, lay down appropriate risk management policies and procedures across the organization.

The Board shall review the Anti-Fraud Policy on an annual basis.

The anti-fraud policy shall broadly cover the following aspects:

i.   Fraud Monitoring Department: Set-up a Fraud Monitoring Department (FMD) with well-defined procedures to identify, detect, investigate and report the fraud. A Compliance Officer shall be designated for this purpose, having direct access to the Board of the company.

ii. Potential Areas of Fraud: Identify areas of business and the specific departments of the organization that are potentially prone to insurance fraud and lay down a detailed area-wise/ department-wise, anti-fraud procedures, risk prevention and mitigation measures.

iii. Co-ordination with Law Enforcement Agencies: Lay down procedures to coordinate with law enforcement agencies for reporting fraud and follow-up processes thereon.

iv. Framework for Exchange of Information: Lay down procedures for exchange of necessary information on fraud, amongst all insurers through respective councils.

v.   Due Diligence: Lay down procedures to carry out the due diligence on the personnel (management, officers and staff) before appointment.

vi. Regular Communication Channels: Generate fraud mitigation communication within the organization at periodic intervals and lay down appropriate framework for a strong whistle blower policy. The insurer shall formalize the information flow from/amongst the various operating departments to FMD.

2. Fraud Monitoring Department (FMD) (Role and Functions):

The FMD shall have in place reporting procedures from the various departments like underwriting, claims, information technology, investments, accounts, internal audit and intermediaries departments. All personnel shall be encouraged to report suspicious instances/ fraud to the FMD.

The FMD shall also lay down the policy framework for the training of personnel and intermediaries to sensitize them on prevention, detection, and mitigation of fraud. Suitable clause should be included in the terms of appointment of employees/intermediaries that clarifies the implications of fraud and penal provisions thereon.

The head of the FMD shall be responsible for furnishing various reports on fraud to the Authority.

3. Reports to IRDA:

Statistics on various fraudulent cases and action taken thereon along with a Compliance Certificate duly signed by the Chief Executive Officer/Managing Director shall be filed with the Authority in form FMR 1 and FMR 2 every year within 30 days of close of the financial year.

4. Reports to the Board:

FMD should lay down appropriate framework for information to be submitted to the Board. The Board shall review the same periodically.

5. Preventive mechanism:

The Insurer shall inform both potential clients and existing clients about their anti-fraud policies. The Insurer shall appropriately include necessary caution in the insurance contracts/ relevant documents, duly highlighting the consequences of submitting a false statement and/or incomplete statement, for the benefit of the policyholder, claimant.